Jack Altman

J·P·M
PUBLICATIONS

C O N T E N T S

This Way Crete

A Place Apart

Fiercely independent-minded, the people of Crete think of their island as a place apart from the rest of Greece. Having fought hard against the Turks to assure unification with the mother country, they seem perfectly happy today to stand aloof, at least psychologically. Inhabiting by far the biggest of all the Greek islands, the proudest Cretans even refer to their home as a "continent".

To foreign visitors, they say, they offer everything they could wish to find in a whole continent—spectacular craggy mountains and pretty green meadows, great beaches, good food and, not least, the cultural treasures of Minoan civilization, the oldest not just in Greece but in the whole of Europe.

Crete owes its ancient development to its position as a trade bridge between three *real* continents: Europe to the north, Asia to the east and Africa some 300 km (200 miles) to the south. Greek mythology consecrates Crete's mixed origins with the story of the Levantine princess Europa being carried off from the coast of Lebanon by Zeus, disguised as a white bull swimming across the sea to Crete. There, she bore him a child, Minos, first king of Knossos. And the proximity of Africa is attested by the subtropical flora you will spot on walks in the island's interior— Crete lies on a latitude further south than Tangiers, Algiers and Tunis.

Shaped like a lazy swimmer floating belly up in the Mediterranean, the island is 250 km (156 miles) long and 60 km (37 miles) at its widest point. Most of its 500,000 population is concentrated along the north coast, where the majority of the resorts are located. The rugged mountainous interior divides into three ranges—the White Lefka Mountains to the west, the tall peaks of Mount Ida and Mount Dikti in the centre and the Sitia Mountains to the east. Their valleys and foothills are green with meadows which bloom with orchids and crocuses in the spring and later with yellow carpets of buttercups. Silvery groves of olives abound, along with orchards of lemons, oranges, apricots, figs and almonds for the city markets, but you will also find these delicacies growing wild.

Midway along the north coast, the island capital, Iraklion, is a busy, noisy commercial centre, flanked by several beach hotels but worth visiting principally for its craft market and grand museum of Minoan culture, before or after your tour of the nearby palace of Knossos. It also serves as a gateway for excursions to other archaeological sites, Phaistos, Agia Triada and Gortis, and their picturesque landscapes.

To the east, Agios Nikolaos, Elounda and Sitia are the principal resort towns, with the most modern and luxurious of the island's tourist facilities. Besides the excursions they offer to traditional mountain villages in the interior and the attractive sandy beaches of Vaï over on the east coast, each of the resorts is within easy reach of the Minoan palace ruins of Malia and Kato Zakros and the Greek Orthodox monastery of Toplou.

The towns of Rethimnon and Chania, built by the island's Venetian conquerors, present picturesque bases for exploring the west coast and Amari valley, nestling against the childhood home of Zeus on Mount Ida. They are also handy for rambles through the celebrated Samaria Gorge and Imbros valley in the Lefka Mountains. Further out on the north-west coast, Kastelli is an increasingly popular beach resort, giving access to more remote villages on the far west side of the island.

At the southern end of the Samaria Gorge are the attractive fishing villages of Chora Sfakion and Paleochora. The only other town of any size on the south coast is Ierapetra, appreciated for its mild climate and

THE BEST WALK The dramatic countryside of Crete's interior offers many an opportunity to stroll away from the all too seductive lazy lizard life at the beach. The most spectacular walking expedition is through the narrow **Samaria Gorge** in the Lefka Mountains, starting out from Omalos after a charming bus or car ride south of Chania. At your own pace, you make of it a hike, ramble or easy-going walk. Along the way, the colourful rocks and pine and cypress groves make it well worth the effort.

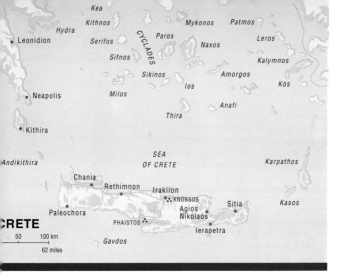

Kea
Kithnos
Hydra
Leonidion
Serifos
Paros
Mykonos
Patmos
Leros
Sifnos
Naxos
Kalymnos
Sikinos
Amorgos
Kos
Milos
Ios
Neapolis
Thira
Anafi
Kithira
SEA
OF CRETE
Andikithira
Karpathos
Chania
Rethimnon
Iraklion
KNOSSOS
Sitia
Kasos
Paleochora
Agios
Nikolaos
PHAISTOS
CRETE
Ierapetra
50   100 km
Gavdos
62 miles

fertile market gardens. Agia Galini and Matala are fast developing resorts.

Fauna, Human and Otherwise

The distinctive personality of the Cretans—tough on the surface, but deep down warm, even passionately so—is the natural result of their long and often arduous history. To the taste for the good life instilled by their Minoan beginnings has been added a tenacious instinct for survival. Invaders from the north—Romans, Venetians, Turks and most recently Germans—have come and gone. The islanders have ultimately prevailed through their strong faith, a fascinating blend of austere Greek Orthodox Christianity and enduring ancient superstition. One of the most gratifying experiences for a visitor is to break through that stoical crust to the cordial smile and hearty embrace of friendship. It is the reward of mutual respect. On your walks along the coast and through the mountains, you'll meet the island's other residents—kingfishers, falcons and egrets, owls, eagles and buzzards, and with luck an ibex, a weasel or even a badger. If they don't smile, it's because they're shy.

5

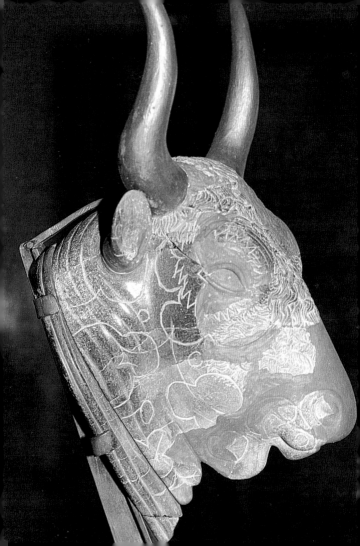

Flashback

Historical Beginnings

Modern Cretans may not like to admit it, but their first taste for the good life came from the southern region of what is now Turkey. For the earliest known inhabitants, a frugal cereal diet was only rarely enriched by wild game. Anatolian farmers introduced the plough and bronze tools to improve the yield of the fertile farmland, put cattle out to pasture in the green meadows, and brightened up the dinner table with olives, grapes and figs.

The island also profited from the settlers' old commercial contacts with the coast of Syria, Palestine and Egypt. Easier living gave the Cretans time to develop artistic skills, and soon after 3000 BC they were already exporting the fine pottery, carved ivory and gold jewellery that were to make Minoan civilization a household name throughout the Mediterranean.

Carved from black steatite, the Bull's Head Chalice from Knossos was the symbol of virile strength.

The Minos Touch

Named by archaeologists after the legendary King Minos, son of Zeus and Europa, the splendid Minoan culture enjoyed a heyday of five centuries, beginning about 2000 BC. The island's population reached some 2 million, four times today's number. The relics of Minoan society reflect a penchant for fun rather than conquest. The palaces at Knossos, Malia and Phaistos were built for pleasure, not to ward off invaders—no defensive ramparts, but plenty of roof gardens, bathing pools, banquet halls and spacious bedrooms. The walls were decoratively frescoed with scenes of games and festivities.

Compared with the gigantic temples and mausoleums being erected for the pharaohs across the Mediterranean in Egypt, the royal shrines of Crete were of smaller, more human dimension, preferring private chapels to massive sanctuaries. The dominant deities were female, represented by petite high-busted figurines with the double axe as their symbol. Their male partners were unmistakably subservient consorts, often depicted as an obedient bull. Their art was a joyous celebration of humour and sensuality. The people of Minoan Crete clearly liked playing around, making love and laughing while they did so.

With the timber of the island's dense forests, Cretan ship-builders formed one of the largest fleets in the Mediterranean. Typically, they used it for a thriving trade in luxury goods to pay for the good life at home rather than turn it into a costly navy for military conquest abroad. Crete's honey, olive oil and wine fetched the best prices, along with the highly prized jewellery fashioned by the island's craftsmen from imported gold, silver, ivory, bronze and precious gems.

Their luck ran out in 1500 BC. Hitherto spared the recurrent invasions that beset the region's islands, Crete was conquered by a strange blond-haired race of Dorians sweeping down from the Balkans. A hundred years later, earthquake flattened Knossos and the island's other palaces. The great Minoan civilization disappeared for more than 3,000 years until rediscovered by modern archaeology. Many of the Minoan Cretans dispersed to the mountainous interior or across the Mediterranean. Some formed the colony known to the Israelites as Philistines, less belligerent and more cultured than their Biblical reputation.

Rome and Byzantium

Crete remained a silent backwater throughout classical Greek history, providing only a few professional soldiers for the armies of Alexander the Great. In 67 BC, the Romans made it a province of their Empire. They moved the capital to Gortis on the southern side of the island. Over the next 450 years, the Roman contribution was above all practical and material—new roads and aqueducts and good plumbing.

Despite the proselytizing mission to the island by the apostle Paul in AD 59, Christianity was slow in catching on in Crete. The people's pagan practices were deeply rooted—surviving to this day in many vivid superstitions that merge with festivities at Easter and Christmas. Inheriting the eastern half of the Roman Empire, the Byzantine rulers only gradually won the Cretans over to the new Orthodox Church.

But the islanders' allegiance was then total, withstanding Islamic rule imposed for over a century by an Arab invasion in 824. The new conquerors established their capital on the north coast at Rabd-El-Kandek

(Candia to Europeans), modern Iraklion. After wholesale destruction of the churches, the Arabs used Crete mainly as a base for piracy and one of the busiest slave markets in the Mediterranean. Byzantine forces proved just as brutal in their battle to recapture the island in 961. The last recalcitrant Arabs were persuaded to surrender when they learned that all their comrades outside the fortress were being systematically decapitated by their Byzantine captors.

Venetian High Life

In the Middle Ages, Crete was up for grabs again when Byzantium lost out to the Crusaders. In subsequent horse-trading, Piedmontese fly-by-knight Boniface of Montferrat picked up the island for nothing and sold it to Venice for a straight 1,000 silver marks in 1204. For the next four centuries, the Venetians made this first of their many colonies the linchpin of their commercial empire. Fortifications at their ports of Iraklion, Rethimnon and Chania still bear the glorious emblem of the Lion of St Mark. Their building was the most attractive the island had seen since the disappearance of the ancient Minoans.

After initially violent resistance to these latest foreign invaders, the Cretans were slowly but surely seduced by the Venetians' taste for refined living. Their daughters found handsome and wealthy husbands, and their sons liked strutting around in those flashy Italian clothes.

The 16th and 17th centuries saw the high point of artistic achievement under the Venetians. Vernacular poetry was distinguished by the romantic epic of Vitsentsos Kornaros. Two gifted painters were born and bred in Iraklion. Michael Damaskinos softened traditional Byzantine austerity with a rich use of colour learned in Venice to create masterful icons for the Orthodox Church. Even more celebrated was Dominikos Theotokopoulos, who also began by painting icons but converted to Catholicism and, after travelling to Italy and Spain, became known to the world as El Greco. In the fierce intensity of his painting, he remained faithful to his Cretan origins.

Turkish Takeover

From the 16th century, Crete became a major stake in the struggle between Christian Europe and the Islamic Ottoman Empire. Extending their power across the western Mediterranean, the Turks attacked the island in the 1530s with pirate raids on Chania and Sitia, 9 launched from Algeria by the formidable Barbarossa Khair ed-Din. The Venetians fended them off and built new fortifications which resisted full-scale invasion for more than a century until first Chania, then Rethimnon yielded in 1645.

The last bastion, the capital Candia (Iraklion), was besieged for 22 years. Heroic Venetian and Cretan forces humiliated successive Turkish commanders, causing one of them to be punished back in Constantinople with public strangulation. After the city was finally captured with the negotiated peaceful departure of the Venetians in 1669, it was calculated that 118,000 Turks had died in the prolonged struggle, compared with the islanders' losses of over 30,000.

For over three centuries of Ottoman rule—until 1898—Crete was stuck once more in a state of obscurity and inertia. Life under the Venetians had often been tough, but by and large bright and colourful, giving free rein to the islanders' creativity. Turkish governors did little more than collect taxes and stifle all cultural life. Rather than build mosques, the island's Muslim community just commandeered churches and replaced steeples with minarets.

From time to time, Cretan rebels hiding in the mountainous interior conducted guerrilla warfare, to which the Turks responded by massacring more accessible farming communities. Even after Greek independence in 1829, Crete remained in the Ottoman Empire. Under the slogan "freedom or death", the cycle of violent rebellion and bloody reprisals continued for another three-quarters of a century.

In the end, the Turks gave Crete its autonomy in 1898 and then full union with Greece in 1913, yielding not so much to the force of the rebels' arms as to the pressure of the European powers.

Greece At Last

It was fitting, and perhaps inevitable, that the Greek prime minister who negotiated the island's *enosis* (union) with Greece was the Cretan-born Eleftherios Venizelos. Fierce freedom fighter on the island, revered statesman on the mainland, he also had the huge task of resettling Greek refugees under the treaties signed with Turkey. In the 1920s, Crete saw the last 10,000 Turks depart, while 13,000 Greek refugees arrived from Turkey.

Throughout this tumultuous period, British archaeologist Sir Arthur Evans was digging into a hillside to uncover the fabled palace of King Minos at Knossos. This unexpected discovery

Sir Arthur Evans's interpretation of the north entrance to King Minos's labyrinthine palace at Knossos.

of a lost civilization, coupled with a growing appreciation of Crete's natural beauty, launched the new industry of tourism. The island's economy also benefited from modernization of its agriculture.

World War II brought yet another invasion. The lightning German advance through the Balkans drove the forces of Britain and its Commonwealth allies to retreat across the Greek mainland down to Crete. Backed by courageous groups of Cretan militia, the effort to resist German capture of the island cost the Allies 2,000 dead and 12,000 prisoners. Remaining troops were evacuated, leaving the islanders to harass the Germans throughout the war with their time-honoured technique of guerrilla warfare.

The bombs and shells of war destroyed a large part of the island's towns, and rebuilding was often carried out with more haste than taste. Today, more care is being taken with new construction in the coastal resorts. The island's natural charm and the great cultural traditions of its ancient civilization are treated with the respect they deserve. The Minoan taste for the fine things of life has not been lost.

On the Scene

You can chop Crete neatly up into three parts—the East, the Centre and the West. The main resorts at the eastern end of the island are Agios Nikolaos, Elounda, Sitia and, on the south coast, Ierapetra. In the centre, the capital of Iraklion does have some good hotels at the beaches on its outskirts, but most people prefer to head further east to the resort facilities of Chersonisos. To the west, resort hotels are mushrooming around Rethimnon and Chania, out to Kastelli Kissamou and south to Paleochora. Excursions to Iraklion for shopping, the museum of Minoan antiquities and a tour of the nearby palace of Knossos can be managed in one or more day trips from either end of the island. To explore the island more thoroughly, it's worth renting a car.

THE CENTRE
Iraklion, Knossos, Gortis, Lendas, Phaistos, Agia Triada, Matala and Agia Galini

A population of more than 115,000 makes the island capital, Iraklion, the fifth largest town in Greece. Lively as it is, this industrial and business centre is too noisy, too close to the airport for a lengthy stay. But if you want to spend a couple of days here, you'll find that the town has a good deal to offer in the way of historical and cultural interest—handsome vestiges of its Venetian past, Byzantine icons in its churches, not to mention the Archaeological Museum, which no one should miss. The high quality of its colourful jewellery and the skill of its ceramics craftsmen also makes it the island's best shopping town.

All in all, rather than planning overnight stays, you would do better to visit Iraklion on day-trips from whichever coastal resort you are staying at, the closest being Chersonisos. The same principle applies for visiting the central region's archaeological sites—at Knossos on the outskirts of Iraklion, and at Gortis, Lendas and Phaistos, further south.

Iraklion

Over the centuries, a conspiracy of earthquakes, the bombs of war and more recent building speculation in hastily erected concrete has replaced the elegant stone edifices that gave the city centre its historic appeal. But you will still find real character down by the port. Serving throughout history as Crete's main bastion of resistance to the many foreign invaders, the town is still known to older islanders as *megalo kastro* (great fortress). This aspect of military defence remains in evidence in the old harbour. (Commercial freighters and passenger ferries are confined to a modern outer harbour.)

Venetian Harbour

The old harbour offers an attractive array of traditional caïques, fishing boats and a growing armada of more affluent yachts. The massive fortress tower out on the jetty was completed in 1540 in face of the growing menace of Turkish pirates. Called *Rocca al Mare* by the Venetians and *Koûles* by the Turks, this was the main obstacle to Turkish conquest during the 22-year siege that ended in 1669. The defiant emblem of the Venetian Empire, the Lion of St Mark, is sculpted on the fortress wall facing out to the Sea of Crete. From the top of the ramparts you get a fine view out over the sea and back across the harbour.

Opposite the Iraklion port authority, tall quayside arcades mark the 16th-century warehouses and workshops of the *Arsenali*. Here, the Venetians performed ship repairs and refitting for trade and warfare in the Mediterranean.

Starting from behind the harbour bus station, take a walk along the top of the Venetian ramparts which extend some 4 km (2½ miles) and provide interesting views of the city's old historical core. On the walls' south side is the Martinengo Bastion (*Promachon Martinengo*) where one of Iraklion's great heroes is buried, 20th-century writer Nikos Kazantzakis, famous for his novel *Zorba the Greek*.

The Major Churches

The churches of Iraklion often reflect the chequered history of Crete in their architecture, switching from Catholic church under the Venetians to a mosque under the Turks and back again 13

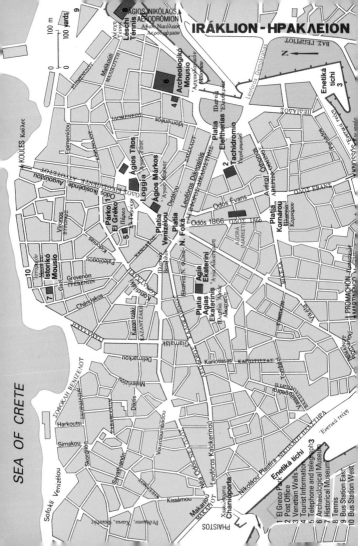

IRÁKLION - ΗΡΑΚΛΕΙΟΝ

SEA OF CRETE

KOÚLES Κούλες

1 El Greco Park
2 Post Office
3 Venetian Walls
4 Tourist Information
5 Telephone and telegraph
6 Archaeological Museum
7 Historical Museum
8 Tennis
9 Bus Station East
10 Bus Station West

- AGIOS NIKÓLAOS AERÓDROMION
- Leschi Tennis
- Archeologikó Mousio
- Platía Eleftherías
- Tachidromio
- Enetiká tichi
- Agios Titos
- Loggia
- Agios Márkos
- Párko El Gréko
- Platía Venizélou
- N. Foká
- Odós Evans
- Odós 1866
- AGORÁ MARKET
- Platía Kornárou
- Istorikó Mousio
- Agia Ekateríni
- Platía Agias Ekateríni
- Enetiká tichi
- Chanióporta
- PHAISTÓS

to a church, but this time Orthodox, under the Greeks.

Typical of this is the church of Agios Titos, behind the arcaded Venetian loggia and City Hall (*Dimarkheion*) in the adjoining 17th-century Armoury. It guards the skull of the island's patron saint, Titus, in a reliquary; he was a disciple of the apostle Paul who brought the Christian message to Crete in the year 59. The skull was only returned to the island in 1966, three centuries after the Venetians took it to Italy when the Turks conquered the island.

In the very centre of town, on the east side of busy Venizelos Square (*Platia Venizelou*) is St Mark's Basilica (*Agios Markos*). Still as Venetian in style as the name of its patron saint, it was built in 1239, converted to a mosque after the 16th-century Turkish invasion and restored to its present form in the 1960s. The interior offers an anthology of Cretan religious art with reproductions of medieval church frescoes from around the island. On the square, dedicated to Cretan-born Prime Minister Eleftherios Venizelos, is the monumental 17th-century Morosini Fountain, supported by four lions and named after a Venetian governor. The square's cafés are a popular venue for political debate.

The most important of the town's churches, south-west of Venizelos Square, is St Catherine's (*Agia Ekaterini*), closely associated with St Catherine's monastery at the foot of Mount Sinai in Egypt. Once a refuge for Byzantine scholars and icon-painters after the fall of Constantinople in 1453, it is now maintained as a museum for the works of one of the greatest of Byzantine artists, Mikhaïl Damaskinos. His 16th-century icons in the nave depict scenes from the lives of Jesus and Mary, subtly combining the cool Byzantine style with the brilliant techniques of the Venetian painters he had seen on a journey to Italy.

KEEPING UP WITH TRADITION

More than most Greek islands, Crete has maintained an unselfconscious attachment to its folk ways. For all its modern atmosphere, you will still see people walking round Iraklion in time-honoured costume, not just the women in their long flowing black dresses brightened only by a flowery kerchief, but also the men in formidable looking boots, bulky breeches known as *vraka* belted with a cummerbund, and above it a billowing blouse and black scarf. These days, the fierce knife is just for cutting bread.

15

Archaeological Museum

Your enjoyment of touring the palaces at Knossos, Phaistos, Agia Triada and other splendours of Minoan civilization will be much keener if you first visit this truly great collection of ancient treasures.

The solid earthquake-resistant concrete block of the museum itself is almost forbiddingly ugly, but the contents of its 20 galleries bring to life the Minoan society's sophistication, richness and energy. Following the sequence of the museum's chronologically organized itinerary (which continues to the Greco-Roman period), here are some of the most important artworks.

The First Palaces (1900–1700 BC): on earthenware tablets, the Knossos "town mosaics" (Gallery 2) depict typical flat-roofed Minoan dwellings, often three-storey with an attic at the top. The famous Phaistos Disk (Gallery 3) with its mysterious spiralling inscriptions on both sides has become a popular emblem of the civilization, manufactured today as gold or silver jewellery or other souvenirs. The tiny figures of birds, animals and humans, more than 200 in all, are believed to represent some kind of religious prayer or hymn, in hieroglyphics which have not yet been deciphered.

Golden Age (1700–1400 BC): the height of Knossos palace's prosperity is epitomized by its supreme symbol of virile strength, the black steatite Bull's Head Chalice (Gallery 4). It served as centrepiece for ritual libations. An ivory statue depicts an acrobat in full flight, taking part in the palace's bull-leaping games. Two high-breasted snake goddesses (or possibly mother and daughter priestesses) are modelled in polychrome faïence. One, with a baby leopard on her head, grasps a couple of snakes, while the other has snakes coiled around her waist and headdress. The merry scenes on the Harvester Vase from Agia Triada (Gallery 7) show that the fun and games were not restricted to the aristocracy—laughing peasants celebrate the harvest in song and dance behind musicians and priests.

The **Hall of Frescoes** (Gallery 14) assembles the celebrated wall-paintings from Knossos. Best known is the seductive, scarlet-lipped *Parisienne,* as she was dubbed by archaeologist Sir Arthur Evans, who found her very chic. A bit too much, perhaps, for the delicate *Prince of the Lilies* who would have felt more at home with the refined *Ladies in Blue.* See, too, the bull-leaping rites in the *Toreador Fresco.*

In towns and villages, the focal point of social life is the kafeneion *terrace.*

Historical Museum

Across town opposite the Xenia Hotel, the *Istoriko Mousio* continues the story of Crete in the Christian era. Its sculptures, paintings, ancient documents, weapons, armour and photographs trace the impact on the island of the foreign invaders—Byzantine, Venetian, Turkish and, in the modern era, German. On the ground floor is a rare early painting of Crete's most renowned artist, El Greco—when still Dominikos Theotokopoulos. His fantasized depiction of St Catherine's monastery at the foot of Mount Sinai was done in 1569. On upper floors are the recon-structed study of author Nikos Kazantzakis, with his desk, books, manuscripts and personal property, and typical rural homes from mountain villages shown with traditional Cretan costumes, textiles and kitchen utensils.

Central Market

Municipal markets are always good places in which to explore a town's typical colours, sounds and smells—and maybe pick up a few things for a picnic. Iraklion's market on 1866 Street is no exception (1866 was a dramatic date in Crete's violent struggle against Turkish rule). Oriental and local spices and 17 herbs set the sensual stage, the fruit and vegetables add the colour and the great cuts of meat and glistening fish heighten the drama. The toothy or toothless smiles of the merchants provide the comic relief.

Knossos

To do them justice, the fascinating excavations at Knossos need a full morning (perhaps followed by a short afternoon siesta). The palace of King Minos is a ten-minute ride south of Iraklion. A walk beneath an appropriately festive arcade of bougainvillaea brings you to the west court where archaeologist Sir Arthur Evans is honoured by a bronze bust. The stone walls on this side still bear blackened traces of the fire possibly caused by an earthquake that destroyed the palace in 1500 BC.

The Palace

The royal residence at Knossos numbered a total of 1,200 rooms, arranged around a maze of corridors, stairways, narrow passages, hallways, small and large courts. As you make your way through them towards the central courtyard, you may begin to feel that this is in fact the legendary labyrinth built by King Minos for the monstrous Minotaur (take some of Ariadne's coloured wool to get back out again). Archaeo-logists have theorized that the elaborate floor-plan was intended either as a potential trap for enemy assault troops (like many a medieval Mediterranean hill-town) or as the intricate itinerary to be followed by priests and worshippers in religious ceremonies.

To the Sanctuary

With the bust of Sir Arthur Evans behind you, turn right to the Corridor of Processions. Here, replicas of original frescoes now in Iraklion's Archaeological Museum show a pair of tawny, curly-haired Minoans in flimsy loincloths bearing ritual vessels towards the palace's inner sanctuary. The sacred route continues left to the southern propylaea, a vestibule of refashioned columns characteristically tapering from the top down. A ceremonial staircase rises to spacious rooms on an upper floor, with a balcony overlooking the palace's central courtyard.

From here, a corridor proceeds to the sanctuary proper. This is no grandiose temple but a series of small, intimate chapels, shrines grouped around a throne room for worship on a personal rather than monumental scale. Even at the height of their wealth and power, the Minoan kings did not share the gigantic tastes of their pharaonic contemporaries. Next

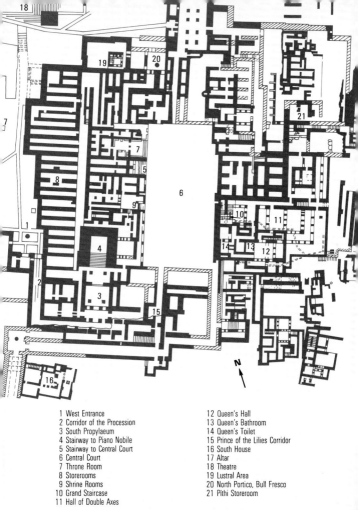

1 West Entrance
2 Corridor of the Procession
3 South Propylaeum
4 Stairway to Piano Nobile
5 Stairway to Central Court
6 Central Court
7 Throne Room
8 Storerooms
9 Shrine Rooms
10 Grand Staircase
11 Hall of Double Axes

12 Queen's Hall
13 Queen's Bathroom
14 Queen's Toilet
15 Prince of the Lilies Corridor
16 South House
17 Altar
18 Theatre
19 Lustral Area
20 North Portico, Bull Fresco
21 Pithi Storeroom

to another staircase leading into the central courtyard on the west side, the throne room is preceded by an antechamber with marble basin for ritual ablutions. The columned Treasury of the royal priests contained the statues of the famous bare-breasted snake-goddesses and other religious objects. Live snakes were probably housed in the adjacent crypt.

Central Courtyard

The main inner court is a veritable arena measuring 26 m (85 ft) in width and 53 m (174 ft) in length. It was here that bull-leaping ceremonies and other ritual sports were conducted. From excavated masonry and frescoes now on display in the Iraklion museum, scholars have surmised that the courtyard was originally enclosed on all four sides. Crowned by emblematic bull-horns, vermilion and gold columns supported grandstand-like galleries for spectators gathered for the ritual tournament.

Imagine the men and women, all wearing ornate but scanty clothing, heavy make-up, elaborate hairdos and intricate jewellery, the women white-faced with scarlet lips and green eye-shadow, the men sun-tanned, their eyes highlighted with black eye-liner. Supporting numbers to the climactic event of the bull-leaping were provided by musicians, dancers, acrobats and boxers.

Royal Chambers

Across from the Sanctuary on the far side of the central courtyard, at the bottom of a staircase, are

---

THE MAKING AND MURDER OF THE MINOTAUR

With a bull's head and human body, the Minotaur is the central figure of Cretan legend. He was the product of a liaison between a bull, god of virility, and Pasiphaë, wife of King Minos. Leery of killing this divine offspring, the king imprisoned the monster in a labyrinth at Knossos and appeased his anger with regular sacrifices of Athenian boys and girls. One of the doomed young men happened to be Theseus, heir to the Athenian throne, who wanted to kill the Minotaur but did not know how to get back out of the labyrinth. Helplessly in love with him, Ariadne, daughter of Minos, came up with the simple expedient of giving Theseus some thread to trace his path in and out. As is the way with busy heroes, Theseus slew the Minotaur, made off with Ariadne and dumped her, pregnant, on the island of Naxos.

the royal quarters. Best preserved of all the palace rooms, four floors of apartments were built into the hillside, two overlooking the central courtyard and two beneath it. A guard room bearing the insignia of shields and the Minoan double axe on the walls precedes the king's chamber (in which a wooden throne was found).

A small passage leads to the queen's chamber, embellished with an ornate fresco of flying fish and dolphins. Her bathroom has a clay bathtub and toilet. The wooden seat has gone, but the flushing system still remains—the plumber is still promising to fix it.

Palace Workshops

Stone-masons, potters, tailors and goldsmiths who worked for the royal household had their workshops inside the palace precincts, north of the royal chambers. Also here are the storehouses for the royal kitchens. Most spectacular are the giant *pithoi*, ornate earthenware storage-jars—for grain, oil and wine—with loops around the rim for carrying-ropes.

Theatre

At the north-west corner of the palace, a second arena provided seating for 500 spectators for dances, boxing, wrestling and other sporting events. This was perhaps reserved for commoners rather than the courtiers using the central courtyard.

DEATH IN THE AFTERNOON

The bull-leaping ritual appears to have shared much of the cruel beauty of modern Spanish bull-fighting. The grace and agility of the athletes might well end in disaster. Excited by the cheering, jeering crowd, the bull would not be reassured by snakes writhing in the hands of the priestess who preceded him into the courtyard to inaugurate the high point of the afternoon with a religious incantation. At his head and tail, two female attendants held him steady. Literally taking the bull by the horns, an acrobat would hurl himself headlong towards the haunches and thrust himself into the air to somersault back onto the ground, facing the bull with his arms aloft. But if the highly-strung bull tossed his head during the manoeuvre, the athlete might be impaled on the horns. Spectators would honour his valour by throwing flowers over his body and perhaps spare him a respectful thought when eating their share of the bull, sacrificed and roasted for the evening banquet.

The Odeon at Gortis was used for music recitals. The Code of Laws is protected by a modern brick shelter.

Gortis

On excursions from the north coast to other archaeological sites of the central region, the journey itself is a great part of the pleasure. The passage over the mountains takes you through spectacular vistas of wild flowers and fertile farmland in the sprawling plain of Messara.

Olive groves and flowering shrubs provide the colourful setting for the remains of Gortis (or Gortyn), which the Romans made their capital in 67 BC. Once housing over a quarter of a million inhabitants, the city encompasses temples, theatres, the agora marketplace, courthouse and residence of the Roman governor.

Inscribed in the stone blocks of the Odeon is the Code of Laws drawn up by the town's earlier settlers from Dorian Greece in 500 BC. Decrees relating to property, inheritance, slaves, adultery, divorce and rape are spelled out in some 600 rows of letters, to be read alternately from left to right and right to left.

Also on the site is the barrel-vaulted ruin (7th century AD) of the Early Christian Basilica of Agios Titos, commemorating the martyrdom of the island's missionary saint and first bishop, a disciple of St Paul.

Lendas

Also known in ancient times by its Phoenician name, Lebena, this pretty little bay lies just south of Gortis over the Asterousia Mountains. It served the Greco-Roman town both as a port and, thanks to its invigorating spring water, as a prosperous health spa. Excavations have revealed the Temple of Asclepius (the god of healing to whom Hippocrates made his oath) and the spa's mosaic-paved Treasury. The springs are no longer operational, but a dip in the sea by the sandy beach of Cape Leon can be just as refreshing.

Phaistos

The superb southern location on a low ridge looking out over the Messara Plain to the Libyan Sea made Phaistos a natural choice for the Minoan kings' winter palace. The ruins reveal a more intimate version of the royal residence at Knossos, maze-like corridors and stairways leading to a central courtyard. A bewitching view greets each stage of your progress, the panoramas clearly incorporated into the architects' plans. Vineyards and olive groves are scattered across the plain watered by the Yeropotamos River. It is cooled by light winds from the north where, behind you, the peaks of the Dikti and Ida mountains are still capped with snow into late spring.

Before reaching the main precincts down a staircase from the north court, you pass on the right an open-air theatre, almost triangular in floor-plan and among the oldest in the world. A second stairway, more ceremonial in scale, rises to the palace's monumental entrance, the propylaeum. To the left, cross the peristyle hall, its column bases still visible, to the royal chambers. The famous Phaistos Disk (in Iraklion's Archaeological Museum) was found in the servants' quarters further east.

Like Knossos, the sanctuary is accompanied by a double-pillared crypt. Stone benches line the walls of the oratory. A large part of the central courtyard has disappeared down the slope, but you can still see the column bases of the portico on the court's western side.

From the sanctuary, a long corridor leads away to the workshops of the blacksmiths and potters. In the storehouses are large earthenware *pithoi* jars for grain, wine and oil.

Agia Triada

On a smaller scale, and so better described as a villa than palace, the Minoan residence is just 3 km (2 miles) from Phaistos. Bearing no ancient identification, it 23 shares the name of a nearby Venetian church of the 14th century (*not* the Byzantine church, Agios Georgios, immediately overlooking the site).

Without the central courtyard of the palaces, the L-shaped construction may have originally served as a country manor for the royal court, or perhaps as a not-too-ascetic refuge for the priesthood. Besides the fine view over Messara Bay, in ancient times much nearer to the villa, alabaster paving suggests a certain degree of luxury.

A five-pillared portico and stairway lead north from the villa to the remains of a village built a couple of centuries later (1200 BC) by Mycenaean Greeks. Around the town square can be seen traces of its shopping arcades.

Matala and Agia Galini

Two beach resorts are close at hand for visitors to Phaistos. The fine, sandy beaches of Matala, to the south, are growing in popularity and the nearby caves are well worth exploring. After being used by the Romans as catacombs, they provided refuges for Christian hermits, World War II gun positions for the Germans and more pacific pads for 1960s hippies.

North-west of Phaistos, Agia Galini is reached by a steep road cutting through the cliffs. This erstwhile picturesque village has sacrificed its charms to the industry of tourism; its hilly streets are lined with concrete hotels and guesthouses. But there are some decent fish restaurants, and you can go out in a fishing boat to escape the crowds.

2 THE TWO MOST IMPORTANT MOUNTAINS They are both associated with Zeus. The god of gods is believed to have been hidden by his mother on **Mount Ida,** south-east of Rethimnon, to save him from being eaten by his father. You can take a scenic drive (and short walk) up to Zeus's cave, which the Greeks turned into a sanctuary. On the east side of the island is the god's cave on **Mount Dikti,** where he grew up on honey and goat's milk. This is a more adventurous climb, but worth the effort for the mountain's spectacular scenery and the cave's stalagmites and stalactites.

THE EAST

Agios Nikolaos, Elounda, Mochlos and Psira,
Gournia, Dikti Mountains, Chersonisos, Malia, Sitia,
Kato Zakros, Ierapetra

East of Iraklion, the craggy views from the sinuous coast road, reminiscent of the *corniche* along the French Côte d'Azur, have won it the name of the Cretan Riviera. Indeed, most of Crete's top resorts and best hotels are to be found in the island's eastern region. An attractive port, fine shopping and good restaurants make Agios Nikolaos the undisputed centre of vacation activity. The hotels' first-class swimming pools make up for the resort's relative lack of sandy beaches. It is flanked by smaller, but not always quieter resorts—Chersonisos, Elounda and Sitia—while Ierapetra remains the major destination on the south coast.

For a change of pace, excursions include trips to mountain villages—some of which, notably Kritsa, still practise traditional handicrafts—and hikes to the caves enshrined by ancient Greeks as the childhood home of Zeus. And there are more archaeological sites bearing witness to the ancient Minoan civilization: the palaces of Malia and Kato Zakros and the intriguing hillside village of Gournia.

Agios Nikolaos

Occupying a promontory jutting out into the graceful curve of Mirabello Bay (*Kolpos Mirabellou*), Agios Nikolaos has almost everything you could wish for in a modern resort town. The year-round climate is a delight, very warm but dry in summer, blessedly mellow in winter. The town is well equipped for all the latest water sports, cheerful and hospitable. Its situation just an hour's drive from Iraklion's airport makes it an ideal base for exploring the rest of the island. The Municipal Beach (*Kitroplatia*) is located south of the bus station.

The Harbour

The jewellery, ceramics and other high-quality souvenir shops are second only to those of Iraklion. They have the advantage of being in a more picturesque setting, sharing the town's fishing harbour with a good selection of seafood restaurants. The harbour is also the starting point for cruises exploring the coastline and little islands of Mirabello Bay. It is linked by a channel cut in the

THE EVENING WALK

At the end of the day, the quay-side promenade past Lake Voulismeni's cafés is the scene of a major social event—the *volta*. This evening stroll is the Greek equivalent of the Italians' *passeggiata*. More than an excuse for enjoying the cooler air just before dinner, it is a chance to see and be seen by neighbours, friends and enemies. It is a moment of genteel street theatre in which everybody is at once actor and audience and people wear appropriately decorous costumes. Younger men and women, no longer chaperoned by parents in this modern era, can display their betrothed. Mothers walk arm in arm lamenting this new state of affairs and share the latest gossip. Fathers talk politics and football.

rock to the pretty little lagoon of Lake Voulismeni. In ancient times, its waters—a surprising 64 m (210 ft) deep—were thought to take you straight down to hell. In the other direction, take the road up to the top of the inland cliff for a heavenly panorama across the lagoon and harbour, particularly fine at sunrise.

Archaeological Museum

In this museum on Odos Paleo-logou, the town has assembled in seven rooms a small collection of Minoan gold and ivory jewellery, bronze weapons, carved shells, terracotta figurines and stone and ceramic pottery from nearby excavations. Among the most remarkable are the 4,000-year-old libation vase known as the Goddess of Myrtos, with its strange lid and spout, and two vases that look uncommonly like a modern frying pan and teapot. A gruesome find from a Roman cemetery at Potamos is a skull crowned with a wreath of gold olive leaves. It had a silver coin in its mouth, the traditional fare to be paid to Charon, who ferried the dead over the river Styx to the underworld.

Elounda

Fast rivalling Agios Nikolaos in popularity, this resort commands the western coast of Mirabello Bay. Besides its modern hotels, many of them nestling in beautifully landscaped gardens, Elounda also has a fishing harbour with well-located quayside restaurants on the jetty. The pebble beaches make a pleasant change from the swimming pool.

Spinalonga Peninsula

From the narrow strip of land immediately north of Elounda,

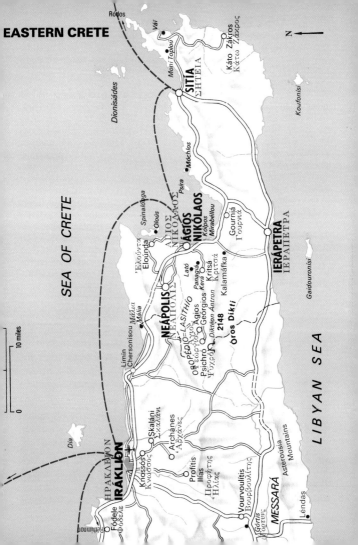

skin-divers can explore the Greco-Roman settlement of Olous, an important city-state dating back at least to 200 BC and now submerged beneath the sea. Remember: report but do not remove any artefacts you might find on the sea bed. On dry land, an Early Christian church has been excavated to reveal a black and white mosaic of leaping dolphins from the 4th century AD. Land-lubbers will in any case enjoy a walk along the peninsula's rugged landscape, popular with bird-watchers.

Spinalonga Island

Elounda (as well as Agios Nikolaos) offers boat cruises out to this island's 16th-century Venetian fortress. At the beginning of the 20th century, it served briefly as a leper colony. On the neighbouring island is the nature reserve of Agii Pandes, where, with luck and good binoculars, you may spot the Cretan ibex.

This endangered species is also to be seen running wild near the Samaria Gorge at the west end of the island.

Mochlos and Psira

Off the eastern shore of Mirabello Bay are two fascinating little islands with the remains of ancient Minoan communities. Like Olous off the Spinalonga peninsula, some of the ruins are partially visible underwater. Mochlos island is barely 150 m from the mainland fishing village of the same name (with a good seafood restaurant). Those who swim out to it should take a pair of thongs or sandals for walking among the dry-land ruins on the island's craggy rocks. For Psira, you have to hire a boat.

Gournia

No swimming, no boat necessary to explore the streets of this ancient Minoan village just 18 km (11 miles) east of Agios

3 THE THREE BEST BEACHES Crete's coastline is generally more rocky than sandy, but you can find some good sandy beaches. The best are at **Chersonisos** on the north coast, where resort hotels have sprung up behind the long stretches of fine sand; out on the east coast to the clear waters of **Vaï** beneath the palm trees; and at the western end of the island at **Kastelli Kissamou.**

Nikolaos. Walls of the houses and shops and the cobbled streets are clearly visible right beside the highway on a hillside overlooking Mirabello Bay. Strictly out of bounds to wheeled vehicles, downtown Gournia kept its streets around the market square too narrow for more than a man or woman to pass with their donkey. Notice the houses' external staircase originally leading to upper storeys. They were probably not unlike traditional houses to be seen in the island's mountain villages today, with rooftop sleeping arrangements for the summer.

Dikti Mountains

To compare ancient and modern Cretan domestic life, visit the villages behind Agios Nikolaos in the Dikti mountains.

Kritsa

This mountain village 12 km (7 1/2 miles) inland from Agios Nikolaos is renowned for the cottage-industry of its weaving. Bed- and table-linen, rugs and shawls are sold in the doorways of the workshops where they are made on the steep narrow streets. The prices here will be slightly better than those asked for in Iraklion or the resort towns. On the outskirts of Kritsa, charmingly situated amid olive trees, is the whitewashed church of Panagia Kera (Sacred Virgin). It is revered for some exquisite frescoes of the 14th and 15th centuries. On the ceiling of the dome are scenes from the life of Jesus. The *Last Supper* is depicted over the nave.

Kalamafka

A short drive inland from the resort town of Istro, this village is popular for its dramatic location on the eastern slope of the Dikti mountains. You can see the Sea of Crete to the north and the Libyan Sea to the south.

Diktaean Cave

This excursion to the childhood hideout of the great god Zeus is strictly for agile hikers. Located 1025 m (3360 ft) above the sea on a slippery path 20 minutes' walk from the village of Psichro on the windmill-strewn Lassithi plain, it has all the stalagmites and stalactites any cave-explorer could wish for. Their strange shapes reminis-cent of Greek gods prompted ancient visitors to erect stone altars and leave bronze votive offerings now on display in Iraklion's Archaeological Museum.

Chersonisos

For the joys of water sports or just lazing around in the sun with an occasional dip in the sea, the long stretches of sand place this among the most sought-after of 29

Crete's beach resorts. It is within easy reach of Iraklion but well away from the city noise. The emphasis here is on the hedonistic pleasures—plenty of bars, even British-style pubs, cafés and discos.

Down in the harbour are the underwater remains of ancient quays, piers and jetties to remind us that for the Greeks and Romans of old, Chersonisos was an important port city for commerce and navy. The ruins of an Early Christian basilica (perhaps 6th-century) perch on a craggy promontory known as *Kastri*. Roman fish tanks are cut in the rock—freshly caught fish would be kept here until needed.

Malia

A short drive east of Chersonisos is the Minoan palace of Malia, built around the same time as Knossos. Unlike the latter, there is no elaborate reconstruction here, just a picturesque set of ruins displaying the classic ground plan of ceremonial staircase, corridors, royal chambers and store rooms grouped around the central courtyard. A major point of interest at the south-west corner of the courtyard is a round

Agios Nikolaos in one of its rare, tranquil moments.

limestone slab known as a *kernos*. The concentric series of hollows grouped like a marble solitaire suggests either a ritual harvest altar for grains and seeds or a gaming table for stones. Behind a raised loggia for sacred ceremonies, stairs descend to a ritual bath similar to the early Christians' baptismal font.

Sitia

This pretty port town at the eastern end of the island becomes crowded only at the height of the holiday season. Otherwise it's a charming alternative to the better known resorts along the coast. Even if you are not staying there, Sitia is worth a visit, not least of all for the spectacular drive along this stretch of the winding corniche road that prompted the name of the Cretan Riviera. The cliffs are dotted with terraced olive groves and citrus orchards, tiny villages clinging to what looks like a suicidally dangerous perch above the sea.

Established as a prosperous trading port by the Venetians, Sitia was a frequent target for the voracious Algerian-based pirate Barbarossa and less discriminating earthquakes. A devastating Turkish blockade left the town in ruins in the 17th century and it recovered only 200 years later. Today it is a popular port of call for boats from Agios Nikolaos. 31

The Waterfront

The harbour offers an attractive collection of colourfully painted houses, shops, cafés and restaurants, particularly lively at the sacred hour of the evening promenade (*volta*). Out in the water just beyond the Port Authority buildings, excavations have revealed ancient Roman fish tanks carved out of the rock.

Archaeological Museum

Sitia's collection includes finds from the region's prehistoric, Minoan and Greco-Roman sites, notably some fine ceramics, a wine press from the Minoan palace of Kato Zakros, and some intriguing ancient fishing materials.

Venetian Fort

With its splendid view over Sitia Bay and surrounding hills, the 16th-century fort provides the stage for occasional summer festivals of theatre and music. Another summer event is the Sultana Festival in August, celebrating the annual harvest of raisins exported from Sitia.

Toplou Monastery

This popular excursion east of Sitia takes you to a 14th-century church left with a Turkish nickname meaning "cannon" (replacing the original name of Panagia Akrotiriani, "Virgin of the Cape"). The cannon is a reference to Venetian military efforts to defend the monastery with added fortifications and artillery in 1645.

Today, the monastery is worth a visit for the much-admired 18th-century icons in late Byzantine style by Ioannis Kornaros (1745–96). Under the collective title of *Lord, Thou Art Great,* 61 scenes glorify Jesus, each labelled by a verse from an Orthodox prayer.

Vaï

A more hedonistic day-trip takes you to the palm-shaded, sandy beach with rocky outcrops out on the east coast. How did the towering groves of palm trees get here? Cretans insist they grew from date stones left by Arab sailors who came here for beach picnics. Nice story, but the trees have been here at least since Roman times and their fruit is inedible.

Kato Zakros

This Minoan palace is isolated from Crete's other royal residences, dramatically situated on the far south-east corner of the island. Its sheltered harbour commanded the trade routes to Egypt and the Orient. As attested by the splendid treasure of ivory and bronze now exhibited at Sitia's archaeological museum, the port commerce brought considerable prosperity. But the town's strategic location also gave it a vital military role in defending the island, probably making Kato Zakros the Minoan kingdom's major naval base. The ancient town of Zakros was uncovered by the British in 1901, but the palace itself, hitherto unknown, was revealed only in 1962 by Greek archaeologists.

The road from Sitia offers a dramatic drive across the eastern mountains' broad plateau and a plunging gorge bordered by green banana plantations on the way down to the Bay of Zakros. The road curves around to approach the palace along the coast from the south.

For an overall view of the site, you may want first to go up to the ancient town of Zakros above the palace. Visitors familiar with Knossos and Phaistos may recognize the classical arrangement of a Minoan palace—a central courtyard surrounded by a sanctuary and sacred immersion bath on the west and royal apartments along the east side. Of special interest to the north of the courtyard are the nicely preserved remains of the royal kitchens—they were excavated with almost all their utensils still practically intact.

The Minoan palace's plan is now believed to parallel, if not imitate, the Egyptian practice of building the apartments of the living on the side of the rising sun and the chapels devoted to immortality where the sun sets. Another Egyptian ritual may be mirrored in the Hall of the Cistern from which a stairway descends to a round subterranean pool 7 m (22 ft) in diameter. Scholars suggest a sacred barque was floated here to enact the king's journey to the gods. Then again, as other scholars suggest, it may just have been the royal swimming pool.

Ierapetra

The only town of any size on the south coast enjoys a mellow climate all year round, a particular joy in the uncrowded winter months. The accommodation available is very reasonable for those on a tighter budget, with a good beach within easy walking distance from the centre of town. The charm of the fishing harbour is enhanced by the well-restored 17th-century Venetian fort built by Francesco Morosini in 1626. A small museum displays artefacts excavated from the original Doric settlement of Ierapytna. Just 300 km (187 miles) from Africa, Ierapetra claims special status as the most southerly town in Europe. Take a caïque to Gaidouronisi, an almost-desert island.

33

THE WEST

Chania, Akrotiri Peninsula, Resorts and Villages, Samaria Gorge, Imbros Gorge, Rethimnon, Excursions from Rethimnon

In the western region of Crete, the resorts are less crowded, but the old charm of the principal towns, Chania and Rethimnon, makes them excellent bases from which to journey into the mountainous interior. They retain much of their Venetian and Turkish character and have fine nearby beaches for water-sports enthusiasts. Over on the rugged west and south coasts, the beaches and offshore islands are delightfully secluded. Sturdy hikers make part of the trip to the south coast via the magnificent gorges of Samaria and Imbros. Even if you don't care about the classical legend associating it with Zeus's childhood, a pilgrimage to his cave on Mount Ida can be a rewarding excursion.

Chania

Beyond the outer town's shapeless unimaginative modernity is a charming historical core that unites the best of its Venetian and Turkish eras. The town that was capital of Crete from 1898 to 1971 stands on the site of Kydonia, an ancient Minoan city mentioned in the stone tablets of Knossos as being founded by Kydon, the grandson of King Minos.

Venetian Harbour

In the graceful sweep of its natural harbour, Chania can claim perhaps the most attractive waterfront on the island. To embrace the whole scintillating panorama, take an early morning stroll around to the lighthouse out on the handsome stone break-water. Come back at sunset and you will see the colours have changed from ivory and buff to amber and gold, deepening as the twinkling lights of the tavernas and boutiques come on for the evening trade.

The port divides into two, an Inner Harbour to the east and Outer Harbour to the west. At the west end of the Outer Harbour, the Firkas, part of the Venetian fortifications, has been restored to house the Naval Museum tracing Greek maritime history with models of ancient Greek triremes and a 20th-century sub-marine. Directly opposite, the Tourist Information Centre has set up shop in the town's oldest surviving Turkish building, the Janissaries' Mosque (*Djami ton*

Private yachts and fishing boats anchor in Chania's sheltered harbour, the most fashionable part of town.

Genissarion) of 1645. East of the mosque, past the Port Authority, the old Arsenals are the most striking feature of the Inner Harbour: seven of 17 barrel-vaulted warehouses that constituted the shipyards for refitting and arming the Venetian fleet.

Kastelli Quarter

Traces of the Minoan settlement of Kydonia were revealed by World War II bomb craters, in what is now the Kastelli neighbourhood rising immediately behind the Janissaries' Mosque. Around Agia Katerini Square, you can still see archaeologists trying to salvage remains of an ancient storehouse or perhaps the royal palace itself, before it is buried once more, this time by foundations for a new hotel or bank. The most important finds are in the local museum.

Topanas Quarter

In the narrow streets behind the Firkas naval museum, the main Turkish neighbourhood is apparent from the "oriental" wooden balconies and mansards built onto the stone houses of the Venetians. Notice, too, the ornate Turkish fountain near the Venetian town gate. Today the quarter is reputed for its fine craftsmen—potters, weavers and carpenters. 35

Shop for a good selection of their work along Theotokopoulou Street.

Evreïka Quarter

Immediately south of Topanas, the old neighbourhood around the Archaeological Museum is now Jewish (*Evreïka*) only in name, but the tradition of leatherwork has continued. You will find the best hand-crafted boots, shoes and sandals on Skridlof Street.

Two Museums

The Archaeological Museum occupies the Venetian church that was part of a Franciscan monastery—in the garden you can still see the Turkish fountain and fragment of a minaret from its days as Yusuf Pasha Mosque. The museum's chief interest is in the ongoing finds of Minoan material from ancient Kydonia. These include sculpture, mosaics and coffins.

On the south-east outskirts of town, on Sfakianaki Street, the Historical Museum contains some fascinating Venetian maps, documents and furniture but constitutes in the main a patriotic homage to Greek, and more particularly Cretan, struggles for independence. A formidable array of weapons accompanies portraits of the island's heroic fighters against both Turks and Germans. Pride of place is accorded to the city's most venerated son, Eleftherios Venizelos. A separate room is set aside for this Greek prime minister born in Chania in 1864.

City Market

In the heart of the modern town, the covered market dates back to 1911, and its abundant stalls of fruits, vegetables, cheeses, meat and fish make it one of the liveliest places in town. It is certainly the best place to encounter the "real" people of Chania rather than just the worthy representatives of the tourist-service industries.

Akrotiri Peninsula

A tour of Akrotiri takes you around a lively ferry-port and out to wild unspoiled countryside which provides a picturesque setting for three monasteries and hermits' caves.

Punching out east of Chania like a giant fist, the peninsula protects the superb natural harbour of Souda Bay. If you come in to Chania by ferry, this is the port of call. The sailors' bars and cafés are appropriately boisterous in the evenings as Souda serves as a base for NATO and the Greek navy. Overlooking the bay is the British War Cemetery for the soldiers who died in the Crete campaign of 1941.

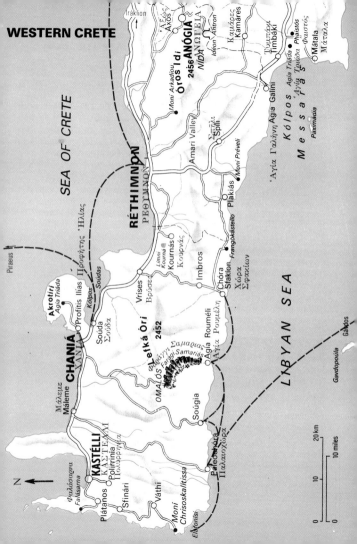

Up on Profitis Ilias hill are the simple tombs of Greek Prime Minister Eleftherios Venizelos and his son Sophocles. They are buried on a historic site of Cretan rebellion against the Turks in 1897. The hill also offers a splendid view over Chania and its bay.

The first of the peninsula's three monasteries, the 17th-century Venetian-style Agia Triada (Holy Trinity) stands out on the limestone plateau with its distinctive cluster of domes, Grecian columns and campanile. It was built by a family of Venetian merchants who converted to the Orthodox Church.

The going becomes a little rougher—and the wild flowers more plentiful—on the way to Gouvernetou Monastery, much older and perhaps dating back to the earliest Venetian settlement in Crete in the 11th century.

Further on, you need good walking shoes to reach the ruins of the Katholiko monastery standing at the foot of a cliff near a bridge. The caves here, with stalactites and stalagmites that proved useful as built-in furniture, were refuges for the earliest Christian hermits.

Resorts and Villages

The beach resorts of Maleme, Kastelli and Paleochora serve as good bases for exploring the fishing villages on the craggy west and south-west coastlines.

Maleme

In the more sombre days of World War II, this now very well-equipped beach resort was a major focus of the German inva-

---

4 THE FOUR BEST MONASTERIES As much for political as for spiritual reasons, the 16th-century **Arkadi** in the Idaian mountains is the most revered of the island's many monasteries, being the fateful centre of Crete's armed rebellion against the Turks in 1866. On the Akrotiri peninsula near Chania, people enjoy the pilgrimage to the 17th-century **Agia Triada** for the wild flowers on the way. At the eastern end of the island, **Toplou** also served as a bastion (for the Venetians), but is appreciated now for its fine icons. On the wild west coast, **Chrisoskalitissa** boasts some admirable frescoes.

sion—Chania's nearby airfield was the island's principal air base at the time. At their cemetery of more than 4,000 graves, just inland from the coastal highway, the Germans have erected a monument to their heroism, still visited by nostalgics of the ferocious Battle of Crete. The cheerful resort hotels, tennis courts and swimming pools make a stark and welcome contrast.

Kastelli Kissamou

This resort's antecedents are the Greco-Roman city state of Kissamos and a Venetian trading post. Today, its most important attributes are the long stretches of sandy beach and the casual atmosphere of its tavernas. It is well worth taking a boat-trip out to the Venetian island fortress of Gramvousa.

The grassy cliffs of Falasarna Bay make a great picnic area, and the sure-footed can clamber down to the archaeological excavations of what was once a prosperous trade port in the 4th century BC. Continue south to Sfinari, a charming fishing village with seafood restaurants and a secluded pebble beach.

Overlooking the south-west corner of the island, the 13th-century church of Chrysoskalitissa monastery has some interesting frescoes—if the door's closed, ask at the local café for the keys.

Paleochora

Growing in popularity, this south-coast town has a bouncing nightlife in its harbourside tavernas and some pleasant little places for an overnight stay. Boatmen will take you out to the Elafonisi islands for a swim on beaches with sands that are pink in hue from the granulated coral. You can also sail to the old pirate's haunt of Gavdos, technically the southernmost point of Europe. It has been identified by scholars as the island where Odysseus dallied with Calypso, while his wife Penelope patiently wove and unravelled her tapestry, waiting for his return.

Samaria Gorge

The hike down the grandiose gorge that plunges through the White Mountains is one of the most exhilarating experiences on the island. To do it right, it's an all-day affair starting out by bus from Chania and on foot from Omalos. This rollicking ramble extends 18 km (11 miles) all the way down to the most welcome of refreshing dips in the Libyan Sea at Agia Roumeli. For the return journey, you take a short boat-trip to Chora Sfakion where a bus will carry you back across the mountains to Chania.

Not-so-secret tip: if you do not feel up to the whole hike, you can still explore at least the southern

39

end of the Samaria Gorge. Take the bus to Choria Sfakion and a boat-trip over to Agia Roumeli. Do this early in the morning, before the first hikers arrive, and the gorge will still be blessedly peaceful.

Omalos

The White Mountain village is the hikers' "launching pad". Have a second breakfast there in one of several cafés. There is drinking water in springs and troughs along the way, but take your own bottle in any case and some energizing fruit and nuts. Your shoes should have sturdy soles for the often rocky path; make sure you have a good hat, as you will not find much shade from the merciless sun.

The Trail

The going is easy enough at first, starting out on a wooden stairway. After hugging the side of the towering chasm of Mount Gingilos, the wooden steps gradually give way to a stony trail. This slopes steeply down some 1,000 m (3,280 ft) to what is not the bottom but only the upper ledge of the gorge. Go slowly, keep to the marked trail and you will have no problem. Things get much smoother once you reach Agios Nikolaos Chapel, nestling amid tall pines and cypresses. The colours of the mountainsides

are a joy to the eye, silver, emerald and Prussian blue. The cool, limpid waters of the pools are refreshing to drink, but obey the signs warning you not to swim in them. The gorge takes its name from the little hamlet of Samaria at the halfway stage, where you might like to cool off in the church of Ossia Maria, built in 1379.

The Iron Gates

Soon after the church, you reach Samaria's most dramatic site, the *Sideroportes* (Iron Gates) where the gorge almost closes in on itself with rock walls soaring 300 m (nearly 1,000 ft) above you. Beyond the "gates", the way is open to the sea.

Agia Roumeli

The beach here, lapped by the gentle waves of the Libyan Sea, is the just reward for hardy hikers. And they gorge themselves on the seafood at the friendly tavernas. Nearby, the Panagia Church shares its site with a Greek temple to Apollo—you can still see in the forecourt the ancient red, white and black mosaic.

Imbros Gorge

The hike here is easier than Samaria, the paths less steep, but the mountainous landscape is just as theatrical, and nature-lovers

Frescoes in Chania's Agia Anargyri church: a Byzantine picture book.

claim that the array of wild flowers in springtime is even more impressive. Imbros is also less popular than Samaria and so less crowded at high season.

Take the bus from Chania to the village of Imbros. The southward hike through the gorge's dried-up riverbed covers a distance of 11 km (7 miles) and, with short rest stops along the way, takes six hours. Just short of the sea, the terminus for the gorge is the village of Komitades. Visit the church of St George here to see the 14th-century frescoes. A bus will take you on the last 5 km (3 miles) down to the sea at Chora Sfakion.

Chora Sfakion

Besides a relaxing dip in the Libyan Sea, the harbour offers some much-appreciated seafood restaurants. But it is the people themselves who are the real pride of the region. Sfakiots are celebrated all over Greece for their bravery—and legendary ferocity—in the guerrilla struggles against the Turkish oppressor. Their great hero in the 1770 rebellions was Ioannis Daskaloyiannis. To commemorate heroic events, many a patriotic Cretan all over the island likes to bring out a Sfakiot costume from his wardrobe—trousers tucked into leather boots, fierce knife in the

41

belt, and a billowing black shirt and kerchief.

Frangokastello

This grand 14th-century Venetian fort is the local focus of Sfakiot heroics. Some 15 km (9 miles) east of Chora Sfakion, its four towers bear silent witness to the insurgents massacred there by the Turkish army. Unpatriotic folk go there to enjoy its sandy beach.

Rethimnon

An atmosphere of old-fashioned elegance continues to pervade the streets of a town that is still a favourite among Crete's small but honourable band of writers and artists. It is here rather than in noisy Iraklion that they meet for unboisterous discussions in the cafés of the older quarters behind the waterfront. This ambience seems to have persisted since the town's golden era under the Venetians in the 15th and 16th centuries and remained largely undisturbed by the Turks. Besides a couple of domes and minarets with which they converted the churches into mosques, the conquerors had the good grace—and characteristic indolence—to add only their delicious coffee. The Venetian tone is recaptured today by an annual festival of Renaissance music and theatre.

The Waterfront

Starting on the east side of the town's historic centre, the Venizelou Promenade follows the gentle curve of the sandy municipal beach. It is lined with boutiques, open-air restaurants and cafés, as popular with tourists during the daytime as it is with the local citizens taking their regular stroll in the evening. At the end of the day, everybody makes their way to the Venetian Harbour, where an old lighthouse looms up from the jetty above the small fishing craft and sailing boats are moored as a picturesque backdrop for the many fine seafood restaurants.

Fortetza

Crossing the promontory of the town's historic centre, Melissinou Street leads west from the rear of the harbour to the Venetians' imposing 16th-century fortress, built and constantly reinforced to resist repeated Turkish assaults, until it was captured in 1645. From their elevated position, the ramparts afford a superb view over the harbour and old city. Besides the soldiers' barracks, artillery and ammunition stores, the precincts originally protected the cathedral, hospital and warehouses for the town's emergency food-supplies and other necessities for a prolonged siege. Of the church, there remains only the shell of its converted form as the Sultan Ibrahim Mosque. The governor's residence still stands near the main entrance. (The Fortetza is the main focus of the summer music festival.)

The Old Town

Inland from the harbour, the combined Venetian and Turkish influences on Rethimnon can be seen in the handsome old houses along Arkadiou Street—now mostly shops or cafés. The overhanging wooden balconies are typical Turkish additions to the arched stone façades of the Venetians. Wander into the peaceful courtyards and you will see stately stone staircases climbing to upper apartments. Where the street comes out onto Petihaki Square, a graceful loggia was once a gentlemen's club for the Venetian aristocracy. Shaded by palm trees, the square continues the Venetian-Turkish marriage of styles with its Rimondi Fountain. The lions of St Mark top Corinthian columns, but the dome is unmistakably Turkish.

Leading south to the town's public gardens is the Venetian stone gateway, Porta Cuora. Minaret and domes still grace the mosque, Djami ton Neranzion, that was made out of the Italians' Santa Maria church. You can climb up to the minaret balcony from which the muezzin's cry used to summon the faithful to prayer. It gives you a fine overall view of the town.

The Museums

The old Venetian prison near the Fortetza serves now as Rethimnon's Archaeological Museum. Its impressive prehistoric collection includes Stone and Bronze Age jewellery, statuary, tools and funeral ornaments. From Minoan and ancient Greek times come sculpted deities and other cult objects, some found in the Idaian Cave of Zeus.

In the Folk Art Museum on Messolonghi Street, the island's traditional arts and crafts are represented by jewellery, woven textiles, basketware, farm tools and household utensils.

Excursions from Rethimnon

Depending on how early you start out from Rethimnon, these three destinations—a monastery, nature walk and cave-hike—can be tackled separately or combined in one excursion.

Arkadi Monastery

Less than an hour's drive southeast of Rethimnon beyond a grandiose mountain gorge, the church and monastic buildings are the supreme symbol of Crete's armed revolt against

43

the Turks in the 19th century. The reconstructed Venetian-style-church with its elegant arched belfry stands in stark contrast to the nearby ammunition storehouse, its roof blown off and the walls of the Refectory still riddled with bullet holes. They bear eloquent witness to the terrible climax of the people's resistance to the Ottoman army. The story of this holocaust is told through its relics in a small museum, together with a cemetery where more than a thousand victims were buried, their skulls still on display in an ossuary.

Amari Valley

This outing, which explores the lower slopes of Mount Ida, south-east of Rethimnon, will please nature- and art-lovers alike. The wild flowers are at their best in the spring, when you will see miniature irises, scarlet tulips and lupins, but amateur botanists will find something to please the eye all year round.

Nestling amid the green meadows and silvery olive groves are many fine churches dating back beyond the Venetian era to Byzantine and even Early Christian times. Platania's Panagia church has some good 15th-century frescoes. Even better, at Thronos, the 14th-century Panagia Chapel has some admirable frescoes combining the austere Byzantine style with more down-to-earth Venetian realism. Outside on the terrace are mosaics from the basilica that occupied the site in the 4th century AD. On the southern outskirts of

---

"FREEDOM OR DEATH"

The brutally defiant slogan of Crete's fight against its oppressors is epitomized by the tragedy of Arkadi. It was here on November 9, 1866, that Abbot Gabriel holed up with guerrilla fighters defending hundreds of women and children from surrounding villages. Overwhelmingly outnumbered by the Turkish army, they awaited the final assault of the monastery before the abbot gave the order to blow up the stores of gunpowder. The explosion killed several hundred Turkish soldiers along with the abbot and Cretan villagers themselves. Religious services still celebrate the anniversary in Rethimnon and Arkadi. The event is watered by tears and wine, the gunpowder recalled by fireworks, and the commemoration ends in exuberant folk-dancing.

Whitewashed walls
and blue doors: the hallmark
of a Greek island.

Thronos, a 15-minute ramble through the fields brings you to the ancient Greek acropolis of Sybrita.

Other notable frescoes are to be found at Monastiraki's church of Arkhistratigos, at Lampiotes, Opsigias and at the town of Amari itself. In a lovely setting buried in the woods, Amari's St Anna Chapel claims the oldest frescoes on the island—dated 1225.

Out in the country near the town of Vizari is the picturesque ruin of an Early Christian basilica (6th century AD). It is worth continuing a little higher to Fourfouras for the view of the Libyan Sea beyond the Messara Plain.

Mount Ida

To Cretans, Mount Ida is also known as Psiloritis, "the tall one", as it is in fact the highest peak on the island—2,456 m (8,055 ft). The mountain's importance to ancient Greeks is that their great god Zeus spent his childhood scrambling over the rocks, wrestling with goats and goatherds and playing around with the milkmaids. You, too, can try your hand at this, but most tours just propose a pleasant excursion to Zeus's Idaian Cave. Though Pythagoras took time off from squaring his hypotenuse to hike up there, a modern road leaves you off at a car park for just a short stroll to the cave. Like Moses on Sinai, King Minos came up to get his laws, and the Greeks turned the cave into a pilgrimage sanctuary. Excavators found jewellery, bronze shields, drums and other votive offerings, now exhibited in the archaeological museums of Iraklion and Rethimnon.

Again, the views along the way are beautiful, with wonderful displays of wild flowers, particularly in May or June around the Plain of Nida up at 1,400 m (4,600 ft). The main town on the mountain is Anogia, frequently destroyed by foreign invaders, notably the Turks in 1822 and the Germans in 1944, but still proudly producing some of Crete's prettiest handwoven textiles—and serving a good hearty wine in the tavernas. Anybody contemplating climbing the whole mountain should start out from Anogia with a guide and reckon on nine hours up to the top and back—perhaps with a night in the summit's chapel to enjoy the sunrise before coming back down.

CULTURAL NOTES

A few arbitrary notes on people and things that have played a part in Cretan life.

Ariadne, daughter of King Minos, was immortalized as guardian of the secret to the Labyrinth at Knossos. Its builder, Daedalus, gave her the magic ball of thread with which Theseus was able to get to her half-brother, the Minotaur, kill him and get back out again. After rotten old Theseus abandoned her on the island of Naxos, she was picked up by the god of wine, Dionysus, who was a lot more fun.

Barbarossa, red-bearded Turkish pirate whose real name was Kair ed-Din, was the scourge of Crete's trade ports from Chania to Sitia in the 16th century. In recognition of his illustrious deeds of plunder and pillage, the Sultan made him admiral of the Turkish fleet.

Candia is the name the Venetians gave to what is now Iraklion. It came to refer to the whole island of Crete and its usage continued, at least for the city, into the early 20th century. The name is an Italianization of the Arabic El Kandek, referring to the ditch or dry moat dug around the town as a fortification after its conquest by Muslims in AD 824.

Damaskinos, Mikhail, was a star of the late-Byzantine school of painters, among whom he is singled out by art historians for his grandeur of manner and feeling for decoration. These are qualities he is believed to have acquired on a journey to Venice from 1577 to 1582, something of an ego trip as he is one of the very few Byzantine painters to have added his signature to his icons.

Evans, Sir Arthur (1851–1941), the "father" of Knossos, arrived on the island with impeccable credentials as director of Oxford's Ashmolean Museum. During his first tentative digs on the hillside south of Iraklion, he won his way into the hearts of the Greeks with some astutely anti-Turkish articles he wrote in the *Manchester Guardian*. This enabled him to spend 40 years excavating the palace of King Minos. Although his energy and enterprise have never been questioned, recent scholars have criticized some of the overzealous "restoration" for imposing Evans's own too-imaginative vision of what he wanted Minoan life to look like.

Freyberg, General Bernard was commander of British and Commonwealth Forces in the heroic but unsuccessful defence of

Crete in 1941. On the testimony of his friend Winston Churchill, this New Zealander who had won the Victoria Cross in 1918 was a man of uncommon personal courage. "When I was staying at a country house with Bernard Freyberg," Churchill wrote in his memoirs, "I asked him to show me his wounds. He stripped himself and I counted 27 separate scars and gashes." He made it a round 30 with the extra three he sustained in Crete.

George, Prince, second son of the Danish-born King of Greece, served as Crete's High Commissioner from 1898 to 1906, when Chania was the island's capital. His major monument is a hunting lodge on the coast, now named Georgiopolis.

Herodotus, father of all historians, describes how Crete twice lost the bulk of its population. The first time was in the catastrophic military expedition of King Minos to Sicily. The second time, three generations later, destiny rewarded their performance as the worthiest of Agamemnon's allies in the Trojan wars by exterminating the people with plague and famine.

Icons are religious subjects painted on wooden panels according to strict criteria laid down by the Orthodox Church, determining both style and subject matter. The most common themes are the *Virgin Mary and Child* or *Jesus Enthroned at the Day of Judgement,* treated in a passionate but austere and often rigid manner. The Cretan painters' exposure to Venetian culture infused their work with a sensuous energy that gives it an added dynamism.

John the Stranger was an early 11th-century hermit who left his cave on the Akrotiri peninsula to spread the Christian word after the Byzantine armies had recaptured the island from the Muslims. Agios Ioannis Xenos is venerated to this day and commemorated every October 7 with a festival that begins at the peninsula's Katholiko monastery.

Kazantzakis, Nikos (1885–1957) is Crete's most celebrated writer, author of *Zorba the Greek* and *The Last Temptation of Christ.* Born in Iraklion of a family of mountain warriors and brigands, Kazantzakis was in turn monk, Marxist and lusty lover of women in his agonizing search for spiritual and physical truth. His own epitaph: "I hope for nothing. I fear nothing. I am free."

Linear Scripts are ancient Minoan forms of writing dating back to 1700 BC. "Linear A" was the name given to a set of hieroglyphics found on clay tablets in

Crete. Together with the more sophisticated "Linear B", a later set of tablets found on the Peloponnese, their decipherment in 1952 provided the earliest forms of the Greek language, shared by Crete and the mainland.

Metellus Creticus, Quintus Caecilius was the man who made Crete safe for the Roman Empire in 71 BC. As so often in its history, it had been infested with pirates who held out for three years against the proconsul's three crack legions. The brigands tried to negotiate a better deal with Metellus's superior officer, Pompey, but were wiped out before they got a reply.

Nikephoros Phokas was the celebrated Byzantine conqueror of Iraklion in 961. It was he who concentrated the minds of his Arab enemies on the idea of surrender by bombarding them with the turbaned heads of captured comrades. Two years later, he became emperor by the simple expedient of having his troops proclaim him so after he married the widow of his predecessor, Theophano. She promptly had him murdered by her lover, John Tzimisces, who became the next emperor. It was this kind of machination that gave the word "Byzantine" a bad meaning.

Odyssey, the journey home of Odysseus from the Trojan Wars, made two stops in Crete: at Paleochora, where the men hunted for goats while Odysseus was fighting the Cyclops monster in a cave; and Gramvousa, an isle off the north-west coast, where the ships waited for a good wind to take them home to Ithaca.

Paul the Apostle may or may not have visited Crete, but in his Epistle to his disciple Titus, a local observer is reported to have said: "The Cretans are always liars, evil beasts, slow bellies." Paul adds: "This witness is true."

Queen Pasiphae is best remembered as the mother of the Minotaur after a brief affair with a white bull—her name signifying "she who shines for all".

Schliemann, Heinrich, famous for uncovering the probable site of Troy and Agamemnon's palace at Mycenae, nearly added Knossos to his booty. He was there in 1886, ten years before Sir Arthur Evans, but gave up his search because he could not agree on the price of the land to be dug up and the number of olive trees to be included in the deal.

Titus was Paul's man in Crete, the island's first bishop. This Gentile from Antioch in Syria was a valuable test case for Paul who 49 managed to get him converted to Christianity without being circumcised. Later, it was Titus's head that proved important after the Venetians carried it off as a holy relic when driven out by the Turks and returned it to Crete only in 1966.

User is the name of an Egyptian ambassador to Crete during ancient Minoan times. It was found inscribed on the fragment of a statue at Knossos and was a key element in Sir Arthur Evans' efforts to establish the chronology of Minoan civilization.

Venizelos, Eleftherios (1864–1936) is the ideal Greek political hero—courageous fighter, wily statesman, fervent patriot, and for a prime minister, astonishingly honest. In this Cretan's campaign to have his native island united with Greece, it helped a little in his motivation to have a first name meaning "freedom".

Wine achieved its greatest fame on the island as Malmsey, a sweet dessert wine originating from vineyards in the Malevisi district west of Iraklion. This major export product of the Venetians played a grim role in Shakespeare's *Richard III* when Duke Clarence was drowned in a barrel of the stuff, "the malmsey-butt".

Xopateras signifies "ex-priest" in Greece and is the honourable nickname of a monk who betrayed his religious oath. He won his countrymen's respect as a guerrilla warrior in the mountains during the 1828 revolt against the Turks. He died defending his family in the Odigitria monastery south of Phaistos.

Yiannaris Khatzi Mikhailis was a rare example of legendary daredevil fighter in the 19th-century struggles who died peacefully in his bed, having served in the blessedly boring post of Speaker at the Cretan Assembly of 1912.

Zorba, Alexander, perhaps the most famous Cretan of all, was really a Macedonian labourer, quite advanced in years when he arrived on the island. He existed only in the imagination of his creator, Nikos Kazantzakis. But the archetypal Cretan peasant, immortalized in 1964 as *Zorba the Greek,* can still be seen sipping an evening *ouzo* at every portside taverna or dancing to a late-night *bouzouki* band.

Shopping

The challenge on any Greek island these days is finding the good quality gift, preferably handmade, among the profusion of cheap and not-so-cheap mass-produced souvenirs. Unless, of course, you have a well-developed collector's taste for kitsch, in which case you will have plenty to choose from. One of the best reasons for spending a day or two in Iraklion is that the capital has the best selection of products coming in from all over the island. A few mountain villages keep up the old cottage-industry traditions, and you may be able to strike a better bargain for craftware bought on the spot in places like Kritsa (near Agios Nikolaos) or Anogia (near Rethimnon). In Rethimnon itself, you can get an overall view of genuine Cretan folk art by visiting the craftwork display in the harbourfront building of the Tourist Information Centre.

Antiques

Officially, anything dating from Greek Independence in 1821 is accorded the status of "antique". To export a genuine antique, you will need a permit—and you're not likely to get one.

Museum shops and monasteries sell very good copies of Byzantine icons; if you want the real thing, Iraklion has several reputed dealers.

Ceramics

Vases and fruit dishes reproduce ancient Minoan styles with vivid scenes from the dancing and bull-leaping of Knossos or classical geometric patterns. The rural tradition continues unbroken in robust oil jars and wine jugs. Look out, too, for nicely reproduced terracotta statuettes of animals and the pagan gods of antiquity. The most delicate pottery, hand-crafted in Iraklion workshops, can be securely shipped for you at a small extra cost.

Embroidery and Textiles

The embroidered shawls and table linen of Kritsa are famous beyond the shores of Crete. But 51 take a look at the textiles of Anogia, too. In all the major resorts you will find nicely finished goods—wall-hangings and bedspreads, pillowcases, curtains, wall-hangings and more delicate handkerchiefs and doilies. Hand-woven fabrics can be bought to be tailored on the spot, made-to-measure.

If you feel like thinking of colder weather back home, the local heavy woollen sweaters, smocks and capes are a fair bargain. Look, too, for the multicoloured woven shoulder bags known in Crete as *vourgia*.

Gourmet Gifts

You may like to take home a last taste of your best Cretan evenings—a box of *baklava* pastry, feta cheese, or a fancy *kouloura* bread to hang on the kitchen wall. Also consider a dry white wine (though *retsina* is not a good traveller), *ouzo* or a bottle of the stronger stuff, *raki*.

Jewellery

You may already be familiar with the intricate filigree patterns in silver and gold, for necklaces, bracelets and earrings inspired by the Byzantine tradition. The more specifically Cretan contribution, increasingly popular, is the exquisite collection of sophisticated models proudly borrowed from the ancient Minoan goldsmiths working at Knossos and Phaistos. These and more modern designs are finely executed in workshops both in Agios Nikolaos and Iraklion. Price is established principally by the weight of gold or silver plus a relatively small percentage for the workmanship.

Leatherware

Styling in leather clothing is at best rustic, more attractive for sandals and shoes than for jackets and tunics. The robust local hides are ideal for bags, satchels and belts, still handmade in villages in western Crete. You can also have leather boots made to measure.

Souvenirs

Lurking behind the shop sign "Greek Art" you'll find a multitude of delightfully kitschy items ranging from bottles of ouzo disguised as Corinthian columns to multiple versions of the Phaistos Disk masquerading as pendant, key-ring or cocktail mat.

All good Cretan girls learn to weave and embroider before they become a bride.

Sports

Water Sports

For family swimming away from the hotel pool, try the sandy beaches of Vaï, Chernonisos or Kastelli Kissamou. But remember, when the *meltemi* wind blows in from the Aegean, pebble and rock-shelf beaches are easier on the eyes than sand.

All the major resorts now provide equipment and instruction for serious scuba-diving and snorkelling. The attraction of Crete's offshore diving is to see not just your fellow fish but the remains of ancient submerged cities and Roman port installations, especially in Mirabello Bay.

Depending on your taste and budget, amenities are also available for water-skiing, windsurfing, parasailing, canoeing and yachting.

Fishing

Hire a boat at any of the resort harbours to go out for the dentex, sea bass or swordfish, and have your hotel prepare your catch for supper. You don't need a licence but the tourist information offices will advise on certain restrictions on underwater spear-fishing.

Rambling

The tourist offices provide detailed maps of the nature trails in the White or Lasithi Mountains. Trekking through the Samaria and Imbros gorges does require some stamina, and if that's your taste you can join up with one of the hiking clubs at Iraklion, Rethimnon or Chania. Climbers wanting to tackle Zeus's lair on Mount Ida (Mount Dikti is easy) can get information about hiring guides and renting equipment from the Greek Alpine Club in Chania. But if you want something absolutely unstrenuous for some quiet bird-watching, stroll across the fields to the monasteries and caves on the Akrotiri peninsula near Chania.

Tennis

The bigger hotels have good asphalt or clay courts, but bring your own racquet. Other hotels can help you with temporary membership of the tennis clubs at Iraklion and Chania.

A spring ramble reveals hillsides cloaked in flowers.

Dining Out

Though its vehemently patriotic cooks do not always like to admit it, Cretan cuisine makes a happy marriage of its Greek and Turkish origins. The savoury variety offers a welcome change from the too often bland "international" cuisine of the hotel's set menu. Meat is served in generous portions. Fish-lovers have a good choice of seafood and occasional fresh-water fish from the mountain rivers. And the island's farmers provide plenty of fresh vegetables and salads. For local colour and meals with the Cretans themselves, seek out tavernas away from the seafront and join the islanders at their later lunch times, around 2 p.m., and dinner starting as late as 9 to 10 p.m. One of the great adventures, following traditional Greek custom, is to go right into the kitchen to see what's cooking before choosing your menu.

To Start With...

For some, the endless array of starters known here as *meze* is a meal in itself, accompanied by a refreshing *ouzo* and water. You can either choose among the dozens of different little dishes available or, if you're a novice, let the waiter bring an assortment of five or six. To save room for a main dish, sample, but do not finish off, every delicacy placed before you. The parade usually begins with olives, black and green, plain or dressed in lemon, garlic, coriander or peppers. Then come the dips—*tahini*, sesame seed paste; *houmous*, chickpea purée; *taramosalata* smoked cods' roe; *melidzano-salata*, aubergines; *dzadziki*, yoghurt and cucumber, with mint or garlic. The stuffed vine leaves are called *dolmades* and pickled cauliflower is *moungra*. Eat these with the delicious sesame bread, *koulouria;* olive bread, *elioti;* or flat unleavened Lebanese *pitta.*

King of the salads is the jumbo *choriatiki salata*—lettuce, sometimes white cabbage, tomatoes, cucumber, capers, black olives, onions, fresh coriander and feta cheese, a meal in itself.

Top of the cold seafood list come *kalamari* (squid) and *okta-podhi ksidhato* (thinly sliced octopus), but also try the *salin-garia* (snails), if you dare.

The hors d'œuvres may also include little sausages made from pork, lamb or veal—*loukanika*, or *tiropitta* and *spanakopitta*, flaky pastry patties stuffed with cheese or spinach.

Popular soups are *avgolemono* (egg and lemon), *psarosoupa* (fish broth), and *fasolada* (bean soup).

Main Course: Fish or Meat?

If you can still manage it, the most common fish dishes, baked, grilled or sautéed, are red mullet (*barbounia*), sea bass (*sina-grida*), swordfish (*xifias*), sole (*glossa*), bream (*lithrini*) or deep fried whitebait (*marida*). Eat your sardines (*sardeles*) baked. Served either plain grilled or in a white wine and tomato sauce, shellfish are more likely to be frozen—spiny lobster, shrimp and squid.

Beef or veal stew (*stifado*) is the most robust of the meat dishes. Besides slices of spit-roasted pork, veal or lamb (*giros*, also known as *doner kebab*), you can have the meat cut in cubes (*souvlakia*). Grilled steaks are *brizoles.* Other lamb or mutton variations are simple chops, bar-becued (*kleftiko*), or as spicy meat balls (*keftedes*). In country villages, you will come across superb dishes made from *katsi-ka*—goat.

Moussaka is also popular— layers of minced beef, aubergine, courgette and spices with a cheese topping. Clearly a left-over from the Venetians, Cretans like good pasta, both cheese-filled ravioli and tagliatelli in meat, tomato and cheese sauces. *Pastitsio* is a rather solid dish of baked macaroni layered with minced beef.

Desserts

Another splendid Venetian leg-acy is the delicate creamy rice pudding, *rizogalo.* The local custard pie (*galaktobouriko*) and ice creams are pretty good, too. Among the local fresh fruit, you can choose from melon, figs, pomegranates, apricots, peaches and grapes. But many prefer, like the Cretans themselves, to leave the taverna for the pastry shop (*zacharoplastio*). There, the Turkish-style pastries are heavenly: *baklava* flaky pastry stuffed with honey and nuts; shredded *kataïfi; loukoumades,* doughnuts in syrup.

Drinks

The beer, locally brewed with German and Danish labels and quality, is fine and the wines are 57

On the way to your picnic, have a look in at the market and stock up from the great sacks of nuts and dried fruit.

more than respectable. Crete claims, as in ancient times, to have the best of Greek wines. The resinous white *retsina,* not quite so acid as the mainland variety, is a taste well worth acquiring, to eat both with meat and fish. (But you may find it does not travel well enough to drink back home.) Among the commonest good dry whites are Minos, Gortis, Logaso and Olympia. Beware of the alcohol-rich red wines (*mavro,* literally "black"); they pack an unsuspected punch, ideal pre-siesta or as a night-cap, but to be avoided by the driver. The Sitia region produces the best of the Cretan reds.

As a sweet after-dinner drink, try the locally produced tanger-ine liqueur, *mandarini.* Besides the aniseed-flavoured *ouzo,* Cret-ans go for the powerful *raki,* similar to Italian *grappa.* Even stronger is the mulberry, *mour-noraki,* distilled in Rethimnon.

If you just ask for a coffee, you will probably be served a watery *nes,* the instant kind. Lovers of *real* coffee should have a thick black *elliniko,* in Crete the safe name for coffee Turkish-style. Served thick and black over its layer of grounds, you can choose it either without sugar (*sketo*), medium sweet (*metrio*) or sweeter (*vari gliko*).

The Hard Facts

To plan your trip, here are some of the practical details you should know about Crete:

Airports

Most international flights come into Iraklion, but there are two other airports near Chania and Sitia serving Olympic Airways and small charter company flights from the Greek mainland and other Greek islands. Iraklion's terminal provides banking, car-hire and tourist information office services, in addition to duty-free shop, restaurant and snack bar facilities.

If you do not have special bus arrangements as part of your package, there are plenty of taxis, airport buses and public transport to take you to most of the major resort towns.

Climate

Like most other Greek islands, Crete gets very hot at the height of the summer, but this is made easily bearable with breezes off the Mediterranean or an occasional retreat up to the cooler air of the mountain interior. In July and August, temperatures may average 29°C (85°F), but in the other summer months you will find a more comfortable 27°C (80°F).

The short rainy season comes in the autumn, mostly in October. Clever people also head for Crete in the winter months when it never gets too cold—Christmas can be quite balmy; some people go skiing up in the White Mountains and come back down to the coast to warm up at the beach. Even in January or February, it's a phenomenal if the thermometer drops below 9°C (48°F).

Communications

To get your holiday postcards back home before you do, disguise them as letters inside envelopes, and the post office will treat them more seriously. Letters and postcards are automatically sent by airmail. Post boxes are bright yellow. You can buy stamps at post offices, in the yellow post office caravans, at newsstands and in the shops selling postcards.

The telephone service is run by the OTE, with offices in all the big towns, generally open from 8.30 a.m. to 11 p.m. It is quite a complicated business to make a phone call, and you may find it more worthwhile using the hotel fax and telephone service. You'll have to pay a surcharge but at least it saves having to wait in line and complicated negotiations should you have the misfortune to dial the wrong number.

Crime

Most Cretans are honest and fiercely proud of the fact. Pickpockets are much commoner elsewhere in Europe, but without undue paranoia, don't tempt the few that do exist anywhere—very often a fellow tourist—with an open handbag or a wallet in the hip pocket. Leave your valuables in the hotel safe. Lock your luggage before leaving it with porters at the airport.

Driving

If you are renting a car, be sure to have a valid national licence or an International Driving Permit. If you have not booked a car back home, you will find local rental firms very competitive in price with the major international companies. Minimum age for rental is usually 21, sometimes 25.

Speed limits are 50 kph in town and 100 kph on the high- way. Drive on the right, overtake on the left, though you may not always find the highly temperamental Cretan drivers respecting this rule.

For most of its length, the north coast highway is in first rate condition, but the hairpin bends east of Agios Nikolaos should be handled with great caution. Inland, there are good secondary roads and a fair amount of bumpy mountain roads.

Electricity

Electric current is 220-volt 50-cycle A.C. for Continental European two-pin earthed plugs. Most hotel bathrooms have outlets for 220/110-volt razors.

Emergencies

Most problems can be handled at your hotel desk. Telephone number for police: **100**; fire: **199**. There is a British Consulate in Iraklion (others in Athens), but consular help is there only for critical situations, lost passports or worse, but *not* lost cash or plane tickets.

Essentials

There's no point in packing your whole wardrobe with you. Clothing should be light; take cottons which are less sticky than synthetics. You won't need much formal wear, but for visiting churches you will need something to cover shoulders and knees. Pack a foldable sun-hat and add a sweater for cool evenings. Good walking shoes are vital.

Include insect repellent and a pocket torch (flashlight)—invaluable for dark Byzantine churches and beach barbecues.

Formalities

A valid passport is all that most of you will need—just an identity card for members of EC countries. No special health certificates are required for European or North American citizens.

Customs controls are minimal at point of entry, with an official import or export allowance, duty-free, of 200 cigarettes or 50 cigars or 250 g of tobacco or 1 litre of alcoholic beverages or 2 litres wine. There's no limit on amounts of foreign currency.

A warning about drugs: be careful about importing certain prescription medication, as these may require an official medical certificate. Codeine has been banned in Greece so check the labels of your headache remedies.

Health

The island's generally good climate means there are no special health problems. Some sensitive stomachs take time to adjust to the Greek diet, but if you don't like oily foods, stick to simple grilled fish or meat and salads for which you fix your own dressing. Unless otherwise stated, it's perfectly safe to drink the hotels' tap water.

As everywhere these days, avoid excessive direct exposure to the sun. Wear a hat, use a sunscreen, and keep to the shady side of the street when sightseeing. For emergencies, make sure your health insurance covers holiday illnesses. Doctors, dentists and hospital staff are of generally good standard, many speaking some English (or German). If you anticipate need of prescription medicines, take your own as you may not find the exact equivalent on the spot.

Holidays and festivals

Crete's public holidays are both historical and religious:

January 1	New Year
January 6	Epiphany
March 25	Greek Independence Day
August 15	Assumption Day
October 28	"No" Day, commemorating Greek resistance to Italian invasion in 1940
December 25	Christmas Day
December 26	St Stephen's Day

Movable:
First Day of Lent ("Clean Monday")
Easter Friday and Monday
Ascension
Whit Monday

Languages

English and German are the most commonly spoken languages after Greek. Street signs are most often written in Greek and English.

Media

European newspapers and international editions of American papers are readily available. Increasingly, hotels have satellite dishes for BBC, CNN, German, French, Spanish and Italian television. BBC World Service radio, German radio and Radio France Internationale are all easily accessible on short wave.

Money

The Greek unit of currency is the drachma. It comes in coins of 1, 5, 10, 20, 50 and 100 drachmas and banknotes of 50, 100, 500, 1,000 and 5,000 drachmas. 5- 10- and 20-dr coins come in several different sizes.

Increasingly, shops and restaurants welcome credit cards and often prefer them to cash. Eurocheques are readily accepted, but traveller's cheques are best cashed at the bank or hotel.

Opening hours

We give the following times as a general guide, always subject to variations.

Banks open 8 a.m. to 2 p.m. for normal business Monday to Friday, but you will often find at least one bank in the major towns opening again from 5 to 7 p.m. and briefly on Saturdays for currency exchange.

Shops are open until lunch time Monday, Wednesday and Saturday. Evening shopping, from about 5.30 to 8 p.m., is usually possible only on Tuesday, Thursday and Friday.

Post offices open in the larger towns 8 a.m. to 7 p.m., but in small towns, they close at 2 p.m.

Hours for most museums and historic sites are irregular according to season and place so you should always check with the local tourist information office. They all close on national holidays.

Photography

Film for video or still-cameras is of course readily available in Crete. If you buy supplies ahead of time, choose film-speeds for the island's brilliant Mediterranean light. Most museums allow cameras, but ask permission. Photography is forbidden around Iraklion airport and in the entire Souda Bay area, site of the Greek and Nato naval base.

Public Transport

There are no trains on the island, but the buses are pretty good, running a regular, quite punctual schedule between Iraklion, Agios Nikolaos, Sitia, Chania and Rethimnon along the coast. Buses are also good ways of visiting all the major archaeological sites and many of the inland mountain villages.

If you are planning a hike in the country, check on bus schedules for the return journey. Taxis, individual or shared, are efficient, honest and reasonable in price.

Social graces

Contact with ordinary Cretans is much easier than you might imagine. In the towns, many speak a few words of English, but a handshake and a couple of words of Greek from you—*parakalo,* please, or *efcharisto,* thank you—can work wonders in getting a friendly response. Remember when you enter a church, modest dress is essential—no shorts or bare shoulders. Keep your swimwear for the beach or swimming pool, not for city streets, no matter how hot it gets. Staring is not considered rude. On the contrary, it is a flattering sign of interest in you, satisfying a harmless, characteristic curiosity, as is asking personal questions about you or your family.

Time difference

The time in Crete is GMT + 2, so when it's noon in London it's 2 p.m. in Crete.

Tipping

It follows the European model with service charges included, by law, in hotel and restaurant bills. You can always add a little when the service has been particularly good.

Toilets

In general, they are good and hygienic, noticeably on public beaches. The ladies' door is labelled *Gynaikon,* the gentlemen's *Andron.*

Most north coast resort towns have a public toilet, but if you prefer to use the facilities of a café or restaurant, it is expected that you will at least buy a token coffee.

Tourist Information Offices

However well organized your trip may be, you can always use a little extra help when the unexpected happens. The Greek National Tourist Office has information centres in all the main resorts.

They provide maps and brochures in English, French and German, particularly useful for ramblers' nature trails, and keep you up to date on those ever-changing opening hours.

63

INDEX

General editor: Barbara Ender
Photos: Bernard Joliat, Konrad Fuchs
Design: Dominique Michellod, Corsier/Vevey
Maps: Falk-Verlag, Hamburg,
p. 5 JPM Publications